W9-BWI-225

BROCK LESNAR

by Matt Scheff

Consultant: Dr. Mike Lano
Pro Wrestling Writer, Photographer, and Radio Host

BEARPORT
PUBLISHING

New York, New York

Credits

Cover and Title Page, © Jonathan Bachman/AP Images for WWE; TOC, © Mike Lano Photography; 4, © Mike Lano Photography; 5, © Zuma Press/Alamy; 6, © Zuma Press/Alamy; 7, © Zuma Press/Alamy; 8, © MarclSchauer/Shutterstock; 9, © Reporter & Farmer; 10, © Ken Wolter/Shutterstock; 11, © Bill Greenblatt/UPI Photo Service/Newscom; 12, © Alexandre Pona/City Files/Icon SMI/Newscom; 13, © Zuma Press/Alamy; 14, © Mike Lano Photography; 15, © Jim Mone/AP Images; 16, © Darryl Dennis/AP Images; 17, © Eric Jamison/AP Images; 18, © Matt Roberts/Zuma Press/Newscom; 19, © Matt Roberts/Zuma Press/Newscom; 20, © Matt Roberts/Zuma Press/Icon Sportswire; 21, © Mike Lano Photography; 22T, © George Napolitano/Retna Ltd./Corbis; 22B, © Mike Lano Photography.

Publisher: Kenn Goin
Senior Editor: Joyce Tavolacci
Creative Director: Spencer Brinker
Photo Researcher: Chrös McDougall
Design: Debrah Kaiser

Library of Congress Cataloging-in-Publication Data in process at time of publication (2015)
Library of Congress Control Number: 2014037331
ISBN-13: 978-1-62724-550-0

For more information, write to Bearport Publishing Company, Inc., 45 West 21st Street, Suite 3B, New York, New York 10010. Printed in the United States of America.

10 9 8 7 6 5 4 3 2 1

Contents

Brock Versus Rock

Brock Lesnar showed no fear as he walked into the ring on August 25, 2002. He had been in the **WWE** for only five short months. Yet in that time, Brock had overpowered every wrestler in his path. Brock had won the King of the Ring **tournament**. He had defeated wrestling **legend** Hulk Hogan. Now, in this SummerSlam match, he was facing The Rock.

Brock is known for his strength and intensity. He is six feet three inches (1.9 m) tall and weighs 286 pounds (130 kg).

Brock's King of the Ring victory earned him his match with The Rock. Sixteen wrestlers started out in the tournament. Brock won four matches to finish on top.

The Rock was one of wrestling's biggest superstars and the WWE's overall champion. Fans couldn't wait for the match nicknamed *Rock Versus Brock*. Brock couldn't wait either. If Brock beat The Rock, he would become champion himself!

Brock gets ready to attack The Rock during SummerSlam.

The Youngest Champion

Rock Versus Brock was a truly wild battle. At six feet five inches (2.0 m) and 260 pounds (118 kg), The Rock matched Brock's size and strength. His **finishing moves**—the Rock Bottom and the People's Elbow—filled other wrestlers with terror.

The Rock slams Brock to the mat during SummerSlam.

The two giants traded big hits and earth-shaking body slams. Neither man would stay down. Finally, The Rock set up his People's Elbow, a move in which he kicks up his leg so he can fall back and drop on his **opponent**'s chest with his elbow. Bouncing off the ropes, he prepared to slam Brock. However, Brock blocked the move. Then, he drove The Rock's face down to the mat with his own finishing move, the frightening F-5. Brock covered The Rock for a **pin**. The referee pounded the mat, "1-2-3." It was over. Brock Lesnar was champion!

Brock prepares to hit The Rock with the F-5.

To perform the F-5, Brock lifts his opponent onto his shoulders, spins him around, then slams him face-first onto the mat. The F-5 is also called the Spin-Out Fireman's Carry Facebuster.

Growing Up on a Farm

How did Brock get so strong? It took lots of hard work! While growing up on a dairy farm in South Dakota, Brock always helped his family with the chores. He would wake up before 5 A.M. to milk the cows. He would try to lift huge bales of hay—even as a five-year-old!

Cows on a dairy farm

North Dakota

Minnesota

Webster

South Dakota

Iowa

Brock Edward Lesnar was born on July 12, 1977, in Webster, South Dakota.

As a teenager, Brock became a weightlifting **fanatic** and the star of the Webster High School wrestling and football teams. He also realized that he didn't want to be a farmer. "I wanted to wrestle," he said.

Main Street in
Webster, South Dakota

Brock had a perfect 33–0 record as a senior on his high school wrestling team.

King of College Wrestling

Brock spent his first two years after high school wrestling and studying at Bismarck State College in North Dakota. There, Brock's height and huge muscles drew lots of attention. His mat skills were just as impressive. Brock's amazing abilities soon earned him a wrestling **scholarship** at the University of Minnesota.

The University of Minnesota is known for its great wrestling team.

Brock's wrestling skills grew at Minnesota, and as a junior, he finished second in the national college wrestling championship. As a senior in 2000, he faced his biggest **rival**, Wes Hand of the University of Iowa, for the same championship. Neither man could gain control until overtime. Then, finally, Brock **outpointed** Wes for the win and the **title**!

Brock (left) battling Wes Hand for the 2000 national college championship

Brock's career college wrestling record was 106–5.

The Next Big Thing

After college, in the summer of 2000, Brock began his pro wrestling career. He started out in Ohio Valley Wrestling (OVW). OVW was a place for young wrestlers to practice and improve their moves. Brock quickly showed he was ready for the WWE by dominating all the wrestlers he faced.

Shelton Benjamin (left)

In OVW, Brock was part of a **tag team** called the Minnesota Stretching Crew. Brock's partner was his ex-teammate from the University of Minnesota, Shelton Benjamin. They won the OVW tag team title three times.

Then, on March 18, 2002, Brock made his surprise WWE TV debut. He ran in from the crowd and jumped into the ring. Within seconds, he overwhelmed not one, but three wrestlers—tossing them around the ring like toys. Brock had arrived. People began calling him The Next Big Thing. Brock truly lived up to that nickname when he beat The Rock at SummerSlam in 2002.

Brock (bottom) battles The Rock at SummerSlam.

New Challenges

After beating The Rock, Brock battled many of the WWE's toughest wrestlers. In one famous **steel cage match**, he hammered The Undertaker to defend his title. A few months later, Brock lost his champion's belt to the **massive** Big Show. He quickly won it back, however, when he slammed Kurt Angle with an F-5 at WrestleMania.

Brock gets ready to toss Kurt Angle at WrestleMania.

The first time Brock was successfully pinned in a WWE match was when Big Show took away his WWE title.

In 2004, after two years as a WWE superstar, Brock began looking for new challenges. First, he thought about football, and tried out for the NFL's Minnesota Vikings. Next, he tried pro wrestling in Japan. Finally, he decided to try mixed martial arts (**MMA**)—one of the toughest sports in the world!

Brock (#69) played for the Vikings during the 2004 preseason.

Ultimate Fighting Champion

MMA is so tough because fighters use skills from many different sports. Some use karate. Others use **jujitsu** or **kickboxing** moves. In MMA, Brock put his wrestling skills and unbelievable strength to work.

Brock at a 2007 MMA event

In 2008, Brock was invited to fight in the Ultimate Fighting Championship (UFC), one of the highest levels of MMA. He lost his first match when Frank Mir forced him to surrender with a tricky leg lock. Brock won his next two fights, however. That earned him a shot at the UFC **heavyweight** title.

The title match wasn't even close. Opponent Randy Couture couldn't handle Brock's size, strength, or skills. The referee stopped the fight in the second round. Brock was the ultimate fighting champion!

Brock (top) battles Randy Couture in 2008. Brock beat Randy to win the UFC heavyweight championship.

Brock remained the UFC heavyweight champion for 707 days—the longest heavyweight title run in UFC history.

Back to the WWE

After eight years away from the WWE, Brock shocked fans by returning in April 2012. In his very first appearance, he knocked out superstar John Cena with a powerful F-5. Then, just as before, Brock battled head-to-head with the WWE's biggest stars.

Brock takes on The Undertaker at WrestleMania.

No match in recent WWE history was as famous as Brock's April 2014 showdown with The Undertaker at WrestleMania. The Undertaker had not lost at WrestleMania in 21 years! Brock didn't care about The Undertaker's record, though. He hit his opponent with not one, but three F-5s. Fans were shocked again when Brock pinned The Undertaker to end his winning streak.

The Undertaker's 21-year winning streak—snapped by Brock—had been the longest in WrestleMania history.

Brock (right) and his manager, Paul Heyman, celebrate after Brock beat The Undertaker at WrestleMania.

A Legend Grows

Brock's incredible win over The Undertaker made him a WWE legend. The legend grew greater after his title match with John Cena in July 2014.

John Cena is one of the WWE's biggest stars.

John was a mighty WWE champion, but Brock made him look helpless. Brock easily won the SummerSlam bout. It was one more championship to add to his list: college wrestling, WWE, UFC, and now WWE again. He kept the title after a furious rematch with John in September 2014.

Brock's fans are glad he returned to the WWE and can't wait to see what his future holds. Every match is an adventure for Brock, and his legend only keeps growing.

Brock has proven to be a pro wrestling legend.

Brock has three children. His daughter's name is Mya Lynn. His sons are Turk and Duke.

The Brock Lesnar File

Stats:

Real name:	Brock Edward Lesnar
Born:	July 12, 1977
Height:	6'3" (1.9 m)
Weight:	286 pounds (130 kg)
Greatest moves:	F-5, Kimura Lock, Backbreaker

Fun Facts:

- Brock was in a terrible motorcycle accident in 2004. In addition to getting many bruises, he broke his jaw and hand.

- Brock has a large sword tattooed on his chest. He got the tattoo to remind him of difficult times in his life.

- Brock needed less than one round to beat his first MMA opponent, Min Koo Sim.

Glossary

fanatic (fuh-NAT-ik) a person who cares very strongly about something

finishing moves (FIN-ish-ing MOOVS) a wrestler's signature moves that usually lead to a pin

heavyweight (HEV-ee-wayt) a large, powerful wrestler; in college wrestling, a heavyweight weighs up to 285 pounds (129 kg)

jujitsu (joo-JIT-soo) a type of Japanese fighting that uses many different holds and throws

kickboxing (KIK-bok-sing) a sport in which two people hit each other with their hands and feet

legend (LEJ-uhnd) a person who becomes very famous for a talent or an action

massive (MASS-iv) large and heavy

MMA (EMM EMM AY) letters standing for *mixed martial arts*, a combat sport that mixes wrestling, boxing, and martial arts such as judo; MMA is often called ultimate fighting

opponent (uh-POH-nuhnt) an athlete or team that another athlete or team plays against in a sporting event

outpointed (OUT-point-id) won a wrestling match by scoring more points than the opponent

pin (PIN) when a wrestler ends a match by holding his or her opponent's shoulders down on the floor for a count of three

rival (RYE-vuhl) someone another person competes against

scholarship (SKOL-ur-ship) money given to people for education

steel cage match (STEEL KAYJ MACH) a wrestling event that takes place within an enclosed metal cage; one of the ways to win the match is to escape the cage

tag team (TAG TEEM) a wrestling event in which two-person teams of wrestlers battle each other; usually only one wrestler from each team is allowed in the ring at a time and teammates switch places inside and outside the ring by "tagging," or hand-slapping, each other

title (TYE-tuhl) a championship

tournament (TUR-nuh-muhnt) a series of games or contests that result in one person or team being chosen as champion

WWE (DUHB-uhl-yoo DUHB-uhl-yoo EE) letters standing for *World Wrestling Entertainment*, the leading pro wrestling organization in the world

Bibliography

Lesnar, Brock. *Death Clutch: My Story of Determination, Domination, and Survival*. New York: HarperCollins (2011).

Matysik, Larry. *The 50 Greatest Professional Wrestlers of All Time: The Definitive Shoot*. Toronto, ON: ECW Press (2013).

wwe.com/superstars/brock-lesnar

Read More

Sandler, Michael. *John Cena (Wrestling's Tough Guys)*. New York: Bearport (2013).

Savage, Jeff. *Brock Lesnar (Extreme Athletes)*. Greensboro, NC: Morgan Reynolds (2012).

St. John, Chris. *Wrestling (Master This!)*. New York: PowerKids Press (2012).

Learn More Online

To learn more about Brock Lesnar, visit
www.bearportpublishing.com/WrestlingsToughGuys

Index